The Complete Guide to AI Frameworks: A Comprehensive Overview

Table Of Contents

Chapter 1: Introduction to Machine Learning Frameworks — 5
- What are Machine Learning Frameworks? — 5
- Why Use Machine Learning Frameworks? — 6
- Overview of Popular Machine Learning Frameworks — 7

Chapter 2: Comprehensive Guide on Machine Learning Frameworks — 9
- TensorFlow — 9
- PyTorch — 10
- Scikit-learn — 11
- Keras — 12
- MXNet — 13

Chapter 3: Comprehensive Guide on Deep Learning Frameworks — 14
- TensorFlow — 14
- PyTorch — 15
- Keras — 16
- Caffe — 17
- Theano — 18

Chapter 4: Comprehensive Guide on Reinforcement Learning Frameworks — 20
- OpenAI Gym — 20
- RLlib — 21
- Keras-RL — 22
- Stable Baselines — 23

Dopamine	24

Chapter 5: Comprehensive Guide on Natural Language Processing Frameworks — **25**

NLTK	25
SpaCy	26
Gensim	27
Transformers	28
AllenNLP	29

Chapter 6: Comprehensive Guide on Computer Vision Frameworks — **30**

OpenCV	30
TensorFlow Object Detection API	31
YOLO	32
Caffe	33
Dlib	34

Chapter 7: Comprehensive Guide on Transfer Learning Frameworks — **35**

TensorFlow Hub	35
PyTorch Hub	36
Keras Applications	37
OpenAI CLIP	38
Hugging Face Transformers	40

Chapter 8: Comprehensive Guide on Bayesian Machine Learning Frameworks — **40**

PyMC3	41
Edward	42
Stan	43

Pyro	44
TFP	45

Chapter 9: Comprehensive Guide on Generative Adversarial Networks (GANs) Frameworks — **46**

TensorFlow-GAN	46
PyTorch-GAN	47
Keras-GAN	48
DCGAN	49
CycleGAN	50

Chapter 10: Comprehensive Guide on AutoML Frameworks — **51**

Google Cloud AutoML	51
H2O.ai	52
Auto-Keras	53
DataRobot	54
TPOT	56

Chapter 11: Comprehensive Guide on Federated Learning Frameworks — **57**

TensorFlow Federated	57
PySyft	58
Flower	59
IBM Federated Learning	60
OpenMined	61

Chapter 12: Comprehensive Guide on Time Series Analysis Frameworks — **62**

Prophet	62
Statsmodels	63

ARIMA 64

LSTM 65

XGBoost 66

Chapter 13: Conclusion **67**

Summary of Key Points 67

Future Trends in Machine Learning Frameworks 68

Final Thoughts 70

Chapter 1: Introduction to Machine Learning Frameworks

What are Machine Learning Frameworks?

Machine learning frameworks are essential tools for anyone working in the field of artificial intelligence and data science. These frameworks provide a foundation for building and deploying machine learning models, allowing users to take advantage of pre-built algorithms and libraries to streamline the development process. In this subchapter, we will explore what machine learning frameworks are, how they work, and why they are important for anyone looking to work in the field of machine learning.

Machine learning frameworks are software libraries that provide developers with a set of tools and algorithms for building and training machine learning models. These frameworks are designed to simplify the process of developing machine learning applications by providing a high-level interface that abstracts away many of the complex details of machine learning algorithms. By using a machine learning framework, developers can focus on building and testing their models rather than getting bogged down in the technical details of algorithm implementation.

There are many different machine learning frameworks available, each with its own strengths and weaknesses. Some frameworks are designed for specific types of machine learning tasks, such as deep learning, reinforcement learning, natural language processing, computer vision, transfer learning, Bayesian machine learning, generative adversarial networks (GANs), AutoML, federated learning, and time series analysis. By choosing the right framework for their specific needs, developers can accelerate the development process and build more robust and accurate machine learning models.

One of the key benefits of using a machine learning framework is the ability to leverage pre-built algorithms and libraries. These libraries contain implementations of popular machine learning algorithms, such as neural networks, decision trees, support vector machines, and clustering algorithms, making it easy for developers to experiment with different algorithms and techniques. By using a machine learning framework, developers can save time and effort by not having to reinvent the wheel and can focus on building innovative and impactful machine learning applications.

In addition to providing pre-built algorithms, machine learning frameworks also offer a range of tools and utilities for data preprocessing, model evaluation, and deployment. These tools can help developers clean and prepare their data, evaluate the performance of their models, and deploy their models in production environments. By using a machine learning framework, developers can streamline the entire machine learning pipeline, from data collection and preprocessing to model training and deployment, making it easier to build and deploy machine learning applications at scale. Overall, machine learning frameworks play a crucial role in the development of machine learning applications, providing developers with the tools and resources they need to build accurate and efficient machine learning models.

Why Use Machine Learning Frameworks?

Machine learning frameworks have become an essential tool for data scientists and machine learning enthusiasts alike. These frameworks provide a structured way to build and deploy machine learning models, making the process more efficient and effective. In this subchapter, we will explore the many reasons why using machine learning frameworks is crucial in today's data-driven world.

First and foremost, machine learning frameworks offer a wide range of pre-built algorithms and tools that can be easily integrated into your projects. Instead of starting from scratch every time you want to build a new model, you can leverage these pre-existing resources to save time and effort. This is especially useful for individuals who are new to machine learning and may not have the expertise to develop complex algorithms on their own.

Additionally, machine learning frameworks provide a level of standardization that is crucial for collaboration and reproducibility. By using a common framework, team members can easily share code, collaborate on projects, and reproduce results, ensuring that the work is transparent and easily understood by others. This standardization also allows for easier model deployment and scaling, as the frameworks are designed to work seamlessly with various data sources and environments.

Furthermore, machine learning frameworks often come with built-in optimization tools that can help improve the performance of your models. These tools can automatically tune hyperparameters, select the best features, and handle data preprocessing, saving you valuable time and effort. By leveraging these optimization tools, you can ensure that your models are performing at their best and delivering accurate results.

Another key advantage of using machine learning frameworks is the support and community that often come with them. Many popular frameworks have active user communities, online forums, and documentation that can help you troubleshoot issues, find solutions to common problems, and stay up-to-date on the latest developments in the field. This support network can be invaluable for individuals looking to advance their machine learning skills and stay current in a rapidly evolving field.

In conclusion, the use of machine learning frameworks is essential for anyone working in the field of data science and machine learning. These frameworks offer a wide range of benefits, including pre-built algorithms, standardization, optimization tools, and community support, that can help streamline the model-building process and improve the performance of your models. Whether you are a novice or an experienced data scientist, leveraging machine learning frameworks can help you stay competitive and achieve success in your machine learning projects.

Overview of Popular Machine Learning Frameworks

The Complete Guide to AI Frameworks: A Comprehensive Overview

In the world of machine learning, there are a plethora of frameworks available to help developers and data scientists build and deploy models. These frameworks provide the tools and resources necessary to streamline the machine learning process and make it more accessible to a wider audience. In this subchapter, we will provide an overview of some of the most popular machine learning frameworks currently in use.

One of the most widely used machine learning frameworks is TensorFlow, developed by Google. TensorFlow is known for its flexibility and scalability, making it a popular choice for both beginners and experienced practitioners. It supports a wide range of tasks, from simple regression to complex deep learning models, and has a large and active community of developers who contribute to its growth and improvement.

Another popular framework is PyTorch, which is favored for its dynamic computation graph and intuitive interface. PyTorch is commonly used for deep learning applications and is known for its ease of use and high performance. It has gained popularity in recent years due to its flexibility and support for dynamic neural networks.

For those interested in reinforcement learning, the OpenAI Gym framework is a popular choice. OpenAI Gym provides a set of environments for training and testing reinforcement learning algorithms, making it a valuable resource for researchers and developers working in this field. It offers a wide range of environments, from simple grid worlds to complex 3D simulations, allowing users to test their algorithms in various scenarios.

In the realm of natural language processing, the spaCy framework is a top choice for many developers. spaCy is known for its speed and efficiency, making it a popular choice for processing large volumes of text data. It offers a wide range of pre-trained models and tools for linguistic analysis, making it a valuable resource for NLP practitioners.

For computer vision tasks, the OpenCV framework is a widely used and respected tool. OpenCV provides a comprehensive set of libraries and tools for image and video processing, making it a valuable resource for developers working on computer vision projects. It offers a wide range of algorithms for tasks such as object detection, image segmentation, and facial recognition, making it a versatile and powerful tool for a variety of applications.

Chapter 2: Comprehensive Guide on Machine Learning Frameworks

TensorFlow

TensorFlow is one of the most popular and widely used machine learning frameworks in the world. Developed by Google Brain, TensorFlow has gained immense popularity among data scientists and machine learning enthusiasts due to its ease of use, flexibility, and scalability. In this chapter, we will provide a comprehensive overview of TensorFlow and its various features, applications, and tools.

One of the key features of TensorFlow is its powerful and flexible architecture that allows users to build and train deep learning models with ease. TensorFlow supports a wide range of neural network architectures, including convolutional neural networks (CNNs), recurrent neural networks (RNNs), and generative adversarial networks (GANs), making it suitable for a wide range of machine learning tasks.

In addition to its flexible architecture, TensorFlow also offers a range of tools and libraries that make it easy for users to develop, train, and deploy machine learning models. TensorFlow includes high-level APIs such as Keras, which simplifies the process of building and training neural networks, as well as TensorFlow Extended (TFX), which provides tools for deploying and managing machine learning models in production.

Another key feature of TensorFlow is its support for distributed computing, which allows users to train machine learning models on multiple GPUs or even across multiple machines. This makes TensorFlow well-suited for training large-scale deep learning models on massive datasets, such as image and text data.

The Complete Guide to AI Frameworks: A Comprehensive Overview

Overall, TensorFlow is a powerful and versatile machine learning framework that is well-suited for a wide range of applications, including computer vision, natural language processing, reinforcement learning, and more. Whether you are a beginner or an experienced data scientist, TensorFlow offers a comprehensive set of tools and resources to help you build and deploy machine learning models with ease.

PyTorch

PyTorch is a popular open-source machine learning library developed by Facebook's AI Research lab. It is known for its flexibility, ease of use, and scalability, making it a favorite among researchers and practitioners in the field of deep learning. In this subchapter, we will dive deep into PyTorch and explore its key features, advantages, and use cases.

One of the main advantages of PyTorch is its dynamic computational graph, which allows for easier debugging and faster prototyping compared to other frameworks like TensorFlow. This dynamic nature of PyTorch makes it particularly well-suited for research projects and experimentation, where quick iterations and modifications are often necessary.

PyTorch also boasts a rich ecosystem of tools and libraries that make it easy to build and deploy machine learning models. From PyTorch Lightning for streamlined model training to TorchVision for computer vision tasks, there are plenty of resources available to help users get started with PyTorch.

In addition to its flexibility and ease of use, PyTorch is also known for its strong support for neural network architectures, including convolutional neural networks (CNNs), recurrent neural networks (RNNs), and transformers. This makes PyTorch a versatile framework that can be used for a wide range of deep learning tasks, from image classification to natural language processing.

Overall, PyTorch is a powerful and versatile machine learning framework that is well-suited for researchers, developers, and practitioners alike. Whether you are working on computer vision, natural language processing, or reinforcement learning, PyTorch has the tools and resources you need to bring your ideas to life.

Scikit-learn

Scikit-learn is a powerful and user-friendly machine learning library that is widely used by data scientists and machine learning practitioners. It is built on top of other popular scientific computing libraries such as NumPy, SciPy, and matplotlib, making it easy to integrate with existing data analysis workflows. In this subchapter, we will delve into the various features and capabilities of scikit-learn, providing a comprehensive guide for those who want to harness its full potential.

One of the key strengths of scikit-learn is its extensive collection of machine learning algorithms, ranging from simple linear regression and decision trees to more complex models such as support vector machines and random forests. These algorithms are implemented in a consistent and easy-to-use API, allowing users to quickly experiment with different models and hyperparameters. Additionally, scikit-learn provides tools for data preprocessing, feature selection, and model evaluation, making it a one-stop solution for building and deploying machine learning pipelines.

Another important aspect of scikit-learn is its focus on model interpretability and transparency. The library provides various tools for visualizing model performance, feature importances, and decision boundaries, helping users gain insights into how their models make predictions. This is especially crucial in applications where interpretability is key, such as healthcare, finance, and legal domains.

In addition to traditional supervised and unsupervised learning algorithms, scikit-learn also offers support for specialized tasks such as text mining, image processing, and time series analysis. For example, the library includes modules for natural language processing, computer vision, and time series forecasting, making it a versatile tool for a wide range of machine learning applications. By leveraging these specialized modules, users can tackle complex problems in areas such as sentiment analysis, object detection, and financial forecasting.

Overall, scikit-learn is a versatile and powerful machine learning library that is well-suited for both beginners and experienced practitioners. Its extensive collection of algorithms, user-friendly API, and emphasis on interpretability make it a valuable tool for building and deploying machine learning models in a wide range of applications. In the following chapters, we will explore how to use scikit-learn in practice, covering topics such as data preprocessing, model selection, and hyperparameter tuning.

Keras

In the realm of machine learning frameworks, Keras stands out as a powerful and user-friendly tool for building and training deep learning models. Originally developed as a high-level neural networks API, Keras has quickly become a favorite among researchers and practitioners alike for its flexibility and ease of use. In this subchapter, we will delve into the intricacies of Keras, exploring its features, capabilities, and applications in the world of artificial intelligence.

One of the key strengths of Keras is its modular design, which allows users to easily construct complex neural networks by stacking together different layers. Whether you're working on image classification, natural language processing, or time series analysis, Keras provides a wide range of pre-built layers that can be seamlessly combined to create custom architectures. This modularity not only simplifies the process of model development but also makes it easy to experiment with different network configurations.

In addition to its flexibility, Keras also offers a high level of abstraction that shields users from the complexities of low-level programming. With its intuitive interface and extensive documentation, even those new to deep learning can quickly get up to speed and start building sophisticated models. Furthermore, Keras seamlessly integrates with popular deep learning frameworks such as TensorFlow and Theano, giving users access to a wealth of additional tools and resources.

The Complete Guide to AI Frameworks: A Comprehensive Overview

Another standout feature of Keras is its support for both CPU and GPU acceleration, allowing users to train and deploy models efficiently on a variety of hardware platforms. This scalability makes Keras an ideal choice for projects of all sizes, from small-scale research experiments to large-scale production deployments. Moreover, Keras supports distributed training, making it easy to scale up training jobs across multiple devices or clusters.

Overall, Keras is a versatile and powerful framework that is well-suited to a wide range of machine learning tasks. Whether you're interested in image recognition, natural language processing, or reinforcement learning, Keras provides the tools and resources you need to bring your ideas to life. By mastering the ins and outs of Keras, you can unlock a world of possibilities in the field of artificial intelligence and take your projects to the next level.

MXNet

MXNet is an open-source deep learning framework that is known for its scalability and efficiency. Developed by the Apache Software Foundation, MXNet is designed to support both traditional neural networks and cutting-edge deep learning models. This framework is particularly popular for its flexibility and ability to run on a variety of devices, from smartphones to cloud servers.

One of the key features of MXNet is its support for multiple programming languages, including Python, C++, and R. This makes it easy for developers to work with MXNet in their preferred programming language, making it a versatile choice for a wide range of projects. Additionally, MXNet offers a high degree of customization, allowing users to tweak the framework to suit their specific needs.

MXNet is also known for its high performance, thanks to its efficient implementation of deep learning algorithms. The framework is optimized for both CPU and GPU processing, allowing users to take advantage of the power of modern graphics cards for faster training and inference. This makes MXNet a popular choice for projects that require fast and accurate results.

In addition to its performance and flexibility, MXNet also offers a range of pre-trained models and tools to help developers get started with their deep learning projects. These pre-trained models cover a variety of tasks, from image recognition to natural language processing, making it easy for users to experiment with different types of deep learning applications.

Overall, MXNet is a comprehensive deep learning framework that is well-suited for a wide range of machine learning projects. Its scalability, efficiency, and flexibility make it a popular choice among developers looking to build cutting-edge deep learning models. With its support for multiple programming languages and pre-trained models, MXNet is a valuable tool for anyone looking to dive into the world of deep learning.

Chapter 3: Comprehensive Guide on Deep Learning Frameworks

TensorFlow

TensorFlow is one of the most popular and widely used machine learning frameworks in the world. Developed by Google, TensorFlow provides a comprehensive platform for building and deploying machine learning models. In this subchapter, we will explore the key features and capabilities of TensorFlow, as well as how it can be used in various machine learning applications.

One of the main advantages of TensorFlow is its flexibility and scalability. With TensorFlow, developers can easily build and train complex machine learning models, from simple linear regression to advanced deep learning neural networks. TensorFlow also provides support for distributed computing, allowing users to scale their models across multiple GPUs and even across multiple machines.

Another key feature of TensorFlow is its extensive library of pre-built machine learning algorithms and modules. This makes it easy for developers to quickly get started with building machine learning models, without having to reinvent the wheel. TensorFlow also provides support for a wide range of data formats, making it easy to work with different types of data, such as images, text, and time series data.

The Complete Guide to AI Frameworks: A Comprehensive Overview

In addition to its flexibility and scalability, TensorFlow also provides a range of tools and utilities for building, training, and deploying machine learning models. These include tools for data preprocessing, model evaluation, and model serving. TensorFlow also provides support for popular deep learning libraries such as Keras and TensorFlow Lite, making it easy to build and deploy models on mobile and embedded devices.

Overall, TensorFlow is a powerful and versatile machine learning framework that is suitable for a wide range of machine learning applications. Whether you are a beginner looking to get started with machine learning or an experienced developer looking to build complex deep learning models, TensorFlow has the tools and capabilities you need to succeed.

PyTorch

For people that want a comprehensive guide on machine learning frameworks, PyTorch is a powerful and popular choice. Developed by Facebook's AI Research lab, PyTorch is known for its flexibility and ease of use, making it a favorite among researchers and developers alike. In this subchapter, we will delve deep into the world of PyTorch and explore its key features, advantages, and applications.

One of the main reasons why PyTorch has gained such widespread popularity is its dynamic computational graph feature. Unlike other frameworks that use static graphs, PyTorch allows for on-the-fly changes to the computational graph, making it easier to debug and experiment with different models. This dynamic nature also makes PyTorch well-suited for building complex neural networks, such as recurrent neural networks and generative adversarial networks.

Another key advantage of PyTorch is its strong support for GPU acceleration. With built-in support for CUDA, PyTorch allows for seamless integration with NVIDIA GPUs, enabling faster training and inference times. This makes PyTorch a great choice for deep learning tasks that require heavy computational resources, such as image recognition and natural language processing.

The Complete Guide to AI Frameworks: A Comprehensive Overview

In addition to its dynamic computational graph and GPU acceleration capabilities, PyTorch also offers a rich ecosystem of libraries and tools. From torchvision for computer vision tasks to torchtext for natural language processing, PyTorch provides a wide range of pre-built modules and utilities to help developers get started quickly. This extensive library support makes PyTorch a versatile framework that can be used for a variety of machine learning tasks.

Overall, PyTorch is a comprehensive and flexible framework that is well-suited for a wide range of machine learning applications. Whether you are a researcher looking to experiment with new models or a developer building production-ready systems, PyTorch has the tools and features you need to succeed. By mastering PyTorch, you can unlock the full potential of deep learning and take your machine learning projects to the next level.

Keras

In the realm of machine learning frameworks, Keras stands out as a popular and powerful tool for building neural networks. Developed by François Chollet, Keras is known for its user-friendly interface and flexibility, making it a top choice for both beginners and experienced practitioners in the field. In this subchapter, we will delve into the key features and capabilities of Keras, providing a comprehensive guide for those looking to harness the full potential of this framework.

One of the standout features of Keras is its high-level API, which allows users to easily define and customize neural networks with just a few lines of code. This abstraction layer simplifies the process of building complex models, making it ideal for rapid prototyping and experimentation. Additionally, Keras seamlessly integrates with popular backend libraries such as TensorFlow and Theano, providing users with a wide range of tools and resources to enhance their machine learning projects.

The Complete Guide to AI Frameworks: A Comprehensive Overview

Another strength of Keras lies in its extensive collection of pre-built modules and layers, which can be easily combined to create unique and powerful neural network architectures. From convolutional layers for computer vision tasks to recurrent layers for sequential data processing, Keras offers a diverse set of building blocks that cater to a wide array of machine learning applications. Additionally, Keras supports both CPU and GPU acceleration, allowing users to leverage the full processing power of their hardware for faster and more efficient training.

In addition to its flexibility and ease of use, Keras also boasts a vibrant community of developers and researchers who actively contribute to its growth and development. This collaborative ecosystem ensures that Keras remains at the forefront of cutting-edge research in the field of deep learning, with regular updates and improvements that push the boundaries of what is possible with neural networks. Whether you are a seasoned practitioner or a newcomer to the world of machine learning, Keras offers a wealth of resources and support to help you achieve your goals and drive innovation in the field.

In conclusion, Keras is a versatile and powerful framework that empowers users to build sophisticated neural networks with ease. Its intuitive interface, extensive library of modules, and strong community support make it a valuable tool for a wide range of machine learning applications. By mastering the ins and outs of Keras, you can take your projects to the next level and unlock new possibilities in the exciting world of deep learning.

Caffe

For people that want a comprehensive guide on machine learning frameworks, understanding the importance of Caffe is essential. Caffe, which stands for Convolutional Architecture for Fast Feature Embedding, is a deep learning framework known for its speed and efficiency in training deep neural networks. Developed by the Berkeley Vision and Learning Center, Caffe has gained popularity among researchers and practitioners for its flexibility and scalability.

The Complete Guide to AI Frameworks: A Comprehensive Overview

One of the key features of Caffe is its modular design, allowing users to easily customize and extend the framework to suit their specific needs. With a focus on convolutional neural networks (CNNs), Caffe is particularly well-suited for tasks such as image classification, object detection, and image segmentation. Its efficient implementation of GPU acceleration also makes it a popular choice for training deep learning models on large datasets.

In addition to its speed and efficiency, Caffe is known for its user-friendly interface and extensive documentation. Whether you are a beginner or an experienced deep learning practitioner, Caffe provides a rich set of tools and resources to help you get started with building and training deep neural networks. From pre-trained models to visualization tools, Caffe offers everything you need to explore and experiment with cutting-edge deep learning techniques.

Furthermore, Caffe supports a wide range of network architectures and layer types, making it a versatile framework for tackling various machine learning tasks. Whether you are working on computer vision, natural language processing, or reinforcement learning, Caffe provides the flexibility and tools you need to build and deploy state-of-the-art deep learning models. Its open-source nature also means that you can collaborate with other researchers and developers to push the boundaries of deep learning research.

In conclusion, Caffe is a powerful and versatile deep learning framework that offers speed, efficiency, and flexibility for building and training deep neural networks. Whether you are a researcher, practitioner, or enthusiast in the field of machine learning, Caffe provides a comprehensive set of tools and resources to help you explore and innovate in the world of deep learning. With its modular design, user-friendly interface, and extensive documentation, Caffe is a valuable addition to the toolkit of anyone working in the field of machine learning frameworks.

Theano

The Complete Guide to AI Frameworks: A Comprehensive Overview

Theano is a powerful and efficient computational framework for machine learning that was developed by the Montreal Institute for Learning Algorithms (MILA). It is known for its ability to optimize mathematical expressions and perform computations on both CPUs and GPUs. Theano is widely used in the field of deep learning for tasks such as building neural networks and training models.

One of the key features of Theano is its symbolic expression capabilities, which allow users to define mathematical expressions symbolically and then compile them into efficient code for execution. This makes it easier to work with complex mathematical operations and to optimize the performance of machine learning models. Theano also provides support for automatic differentiation, making it easier to compute gradients and optimize models during training.

In addition to its symbolic expression capabilities, Theano also offers a variety of optimization techniques to improve the performance of machine learning models. These include automatic loop optimization, memory optimization, and parallelization techniques. By taking advantage of these optimizations, users can speed up the training process and improve the accuracy of their models.

Another benefit of using Theano is its compatibility with other popular machine learning libraries and frameworks, such as TensorFlow and Keras. This allows users to easily integrate Theano into their existing workflows and take advantage of its powerful features alongside other tools. Additionally, Theano is open-source and actively maintained by the machine learning community, ensuring that it continues to evolve and improve over time.

Overall, Theano is a versatile and powerful tool for building and training machine learning models. Whether you are working on deep learning, reinforcement learning, natural language processing, computer vision, or any other machine learning task, Theano can help you optimize your models and achieve better results. By mastering the capabilities of Theano, you can take your machine learning projects to the next level and stay at the forefront of the field.

Chapter 4: Comprehensive Guide on Reinforcement Learning Frameworks

OpenAI Gym

OpenAI Gym is a widely used toolkit for developing and comparing reinforcement learning algorithms. It provides a variety of environments for testing different reinforcement learning agents, making it a valuable resource for researchers and developers in the field. OpenAI Gym is designed to be easy to use and flexible, allowing users to quickly set up experiments and iterate on their algorithms.

One of the key features of OpenAI Gym is its extensive collection of environments, which cover a wide range of tasks from simple grid worlds to complex physics simulations. This allows users to test their algorithms on a diverse set of challenges, helping them to understand the strengths and weaknesses of different approaches. Additionally, OpenAI Gym provides a standardized interface for interacting with these environments, making it easy to swap out different algorithms and compare their performance.

Another important aspect of OpenAI Gym is its support for multiple programming languages, including Python and C++. This makes it accessible to a wide audience of developers, regardless of their preferred language. In addition, OpenAI Gym integrates seamlessly with popular machine learning libraries such as TensorFlow and PyTorch, allowing users to leverage their existing knowledge and tools when working with reinforcement learning.

OpenAI Gym also includes a number of tools for visualizing and analyzing the performance of reinforcement learning agents. This can be invaluable for debugging and fine-tuning algorithms, helping users to understand what is working well and where improvements can be made. By providing these tools, OpenAI Gym helps to streamline the development process and accelerate progress in the field of reinforcement learning.

Overall, OpenAI Gym is a powerful and versatile toolkit for anyone looking to explore the world of reinforcement learning. Whether you are a researcher, developer, or hobbyist, OpenAI Gym provides the tools and resources you need to experiment with different algorithms and environments, and ultimately push the boundaries of what is possible in the field of machine learning.

RLlib

RLlib, short for Reinforcement Learning Library, is an open-source library developed by the team at Berkeley AI Research (BAIR) to facilitate the implementation and testing of reinforcement learning algorithms. RLlib provides a comprehensive set of tools and utilities that make it easy for researchers and developers to experiment with different reinforcement learning algorithms and models. This subchapter will provide an overview of RLlib and its key features, as well as some examples of how it can be used in practice.

One of the key features of RLlib is its support for a wide range of reinforcement learning algorithms, including both traditional algorithms like Q-learning and policy gradient methods, as well as more recent advances such as deep reinforcement learning and hierarchical reinforcement learning. This makes RLlib a versatile tool that can be used for a variety of different tasks and applications, from simple grid-world environments to complex video games and robotics tasks.

In addition to its support for a wide range of algorithms, RLlib also provides a number of utilities and tools that make it easy to train and evaluate reinforcement learning models. These include built-in support for parallelized training, distributed training across multiple machines, and integration with popular deep learning frameworks like TensorFlow and PyTorch. This makes it easy to scale up reinforcement learning experiments and run them on large-scale computing clusters.

Another key feature of RLlib is its support for custom environments and reward functions, which allows researchers and developers to easily experiment with different environments and tasks. RLlib provides a simple and flexible interface for defining custom environments and reward functions, making it easy to adapt existing algorithms to new tasks or create entirely new algorithms from scratch.

Overall, RLlib is a powerful and versatile library that provides a comprehensive set of tools and utilities for researching and developing reinforcement learning algorithms. Whether you are a seasoned researcher looking to experiment with the latest advances in reinforcement learning, or a developer looking to incorporate reinforcement learning into your applications, RLlib has something to offer for everyone.

Keras-RL

In the world of machine learning frameworks, Keras-RL stands out as a powerful tool for implementing reinforcement learning algorithms. This subchapter will provide a comprehensive guide to Keras-RL for those looking to delve deeper into the world of reinforcement learning.

Keras-RL is a high-level interface built on top of Keras, a popular deep learning library. It provides a simple and intuitive way to implement reinforcement learning algorithms, making it ideal for both beginners and experienced practitioners. With Keras-RL, users can easily train and test reinforcement learning agents in a variety of environments.

One of the key features of Keras-RL is its modular design, which allows users to customize and extend the library to suit their specific needs. Whether you are working on a simple grid world problem or a complex robotic control task, Keras-RL provides the flexibility and scalability needed to tackle a wide range of reinforcement learning challenges.

In addition to its flexibility, Keras-RL also offers a wide range of pre-built reinforcement learning algorithms, including Deep Q-Networks (DQN), Proximal Policy Optimization (PPO), and Actor-Critic methods. These algorithms are implemented in a clean and efficient manner, making it easy for users to experiment with different approaches and evaluate their performance.

Overall, Keras-RL is a valuable addition to the toolkit of any machine learning practitioner interested in reinforcement learning. With its user-friendly interface, modular design, and wide range of pre-built algorithms, Keras-RL provides a solid foundation for exploring the exciting field of reinforcement learning. Whether you are a beginner or an experienced researcher, Keras-RL has something to offer for everyone in the realm of machine learning frameworks.

Stable Baselines

Stable baselines are a crucial component of machine learning frameworks, providing a solid foundation for building and training models. In this subchapter, we will explore the importance of stable baselines in machine learning and how they contribute to the overall performance and reliability of models.

One of the key benefits of using stable baselines is that they help to ensure consistent and reliable results across different runs of the same model. By providing a stable starting point for training, baselines help to reduce variability in the training process and improve the reproducibility of results.

Additionally, stable baselines can help to prevent overfitting by providing a solid foundation for model training. By starting with a stable baseline, models are less likely to memorize the training data and more likely to generalize well to new, unseen data.

In the context of deep learning frameworks, stable baselines are particularly important for ensuring the stability of the training process. Deep learning models are highly complex and can be prone to instability during training, making it essential to start with a stable baseline to prevent training from diverging or getting stuck in local minima.

Overall, stable baselines play a critical role in ensuring the reliability and performance of machine learning models. By providing a solid foundation for training, baselines help to reduce variability, prevent overfitting, and improve the stability of the training process. For those looking to build robust and reliable machine learning models, understanding and utilizing stable baselines is essential.

Dopamine

Dopamine is a crucial neurotransmitter that plays a significant role in the brain's reward system. It is often referred to as the "feel-good" chemical because it is released in response to pleasurable experiences. Dopamine is involved in various functions such as motivation, reinforcement, and motor control. In the context of machine learning, dopamine is often associated with the concept of reinforcement learning, where agents learn to take actions to maximize rewards.

In the realm of machine learning frameworks, dopamine has inspired the development of a reinforcement learning framework of the same name. The Dopamine framework, developed by Google Research, provides a flexible and modular platform for training and evaluating reinforcement learning algorithms. It offers a range of state-of-the-art algorithms, such as DQN and Rainbow, along with tools for visualizing and analyzing agent performance.

One of the key features of the Dopamine framework is its emphasis on reproducibility and research transparency. It provides a standardized interface for defining environments, agents, and training procedures, making it easy to compare results across different experiments. This transparency is essential for advancing the field of reinforcement learning and ensuring that research findings are reliable and replicable.

In addition to its flexibility and transparency, the Dopamine framework also offers a user-friendly API that simplifies the process of implementing and experimenting with reinforcement learning algorithms. This accessibility makes it an ideal choice for both researchers and practitioners looking to explore the capabilities of reinforcement learning in their projects. By leveraging the power of dopamine, users can unlock new possibilities in machine learning and artificial intelligence.

Overall, dopamine serves as a powerful metaphor for the rewards and motivations that drive progress in the field of machine learning frameworks. By incorporating principles of reinforcement learning and reward maximization, frameworks like Dopamine are pushing the boundaries of what is possible in AI research. With its comprehensive set of tools and algorithms, the Dopamine framework is a valuable resource for anyone seeking to delve deeper into the world of reinforcement learning and harness the potential of dopamine for advancing their projects.

Chapter 5: Comprehensive Guide on Natural Language Processing Frameworks

NLTK

In the realm of natural language processing (NLP), the Natural Language Toolkit, or NLTK, stands out as a powerful and flexible framework for text processing and analysis. Developed by researchers at the University of Pennsylvania, NLTK provides a wide range of tools and resources for tasks such as tokenization, stemming, tagging, parsing, and more. For people that want a comprehensive guide on NLP frameworks, NLTK is a must-have in their toolkit.

One of the key features of NLTK is its extensive collection of corpora and lexical resources, which cover a wide range of languages and text genres. These resources enable users to easily access and manipulate large amounts of text data for training and testing various NLP models. Additionally, NLTK provides a number of pre-trained models and algorithms for common NLP tasks, such as named entity recognition, sentiment analysis, and part-of-speech tagging.

NLTK also offers a range of tools for text processing and analysis, including modules for text classification, information retrieval, and text generation. These tools can be easily integrated into machine learning pipelines for building and deploying NLP models. Furthermore, NLTK provides support for popular NLP libraries such as WordNet and the Stanford NLP toolkit, allowing users to leverage additional resources and functionalities.

For those looking to delve deeper into the world of NLP, NLTK offers comprehensive documentation and tutorials that cover a wide range of topics, from basic text processing techniques to advanced machine learning algorithms. This makes it an ideal framework for both beginners and experts in the field of natural language processing. With its rich set of features and resources, NLTK is a versatile framework that can be used for a wide range of NLP applications, from sentiment analysis and text summarization to machine translation and question answering.

In conclusion, NLTK is a comprehensive and powerful framework for natural language processing that provides a wide range of tools and resources for text processing and analysis. Whether you are a beginner looking to get started in NLP or an expert seeking to enhance your models with advanced algorithms, NLTK has something to offer for everyone. With its user-friendly interface, extensive documentation, and active community support, NLTK is a valuable asset for anyone working in the field of natural language processing.

SpaCy

SpaCy is a powerful and efficient natural language processing (NLP) library that is gaining popularity among data scientists and machine learning practitioners. In this subchapter, we will explore the key features and capabilities of SpaCy, as well as how it can be used in various applications.

One of the standout features of SpaCy is its pre-trained models for different languages, which allows users to perform tasks such as tokenization, part-of-speech tagging, named entity recognition, and dependency parsing with ease. These models are trained on large corpora of text data, making them highly accurate and reliable for NLP tasks.

Another advantage of SpaCy is its speed and efficiency, as it is optimized for performance and can process large volumes of text data quickly. This makes it ideal for real-time applications where speed is crucial, such as chatbots, sentiment analysis, and text classification.

SpaCy also provides a user-friendly interface and extensive documentation, making it easy for both beginners and experienced users to get started with NLP tasks. Its API is well-designed and intuitive, allowing users to perform complex NLP tasks with just a few lines of code.

Overall, SpaCy is a comprehensive and versatile NLP library that is well-suited for a wide range of applications in the fields of machine learning, deep learning, natural language processing, and more. Whether you are a seasoned data scientist or just starting out in the world of NLP, SpaCy is definitely worth exploring for your next project.

Gensim

Gensim is a popular open-source Python library for natural language processing and topic modeling. It is widely used for tasks such as document similarity analysis, text summarization, and keyword extraction. Gensim provides tools and algorithms for building and training word embeddings models, which are essential for many NLP tasks.

One of the key features of Gensim is its implementation of the Word2Vec algorithm, which is used to create word embeddings by learning the relationships between words in a large corpus of text. These word embeddings can then be used to represent words as dense vectors in a high-dimensional space, capturing semantic relationships between words.

Gensim also offers implementations of other popular algorithms such as Latent Semantic Analysis (LSA) and Latent Dirichlet Allocation (LDA) for topic modeling. These algorithms can be used to discover latent topics in a collection of documents and extract meaningful insights from text data.

In addition to its text processing capabilities, Gensim also provides tools for working with other types of data, such as time series and network data. It offers algorithms for similarity analysis, clustering, and dimensionality reduction, making it a versatile tool for a wide range of machine learning tasks.

Overall, Gensim is a powerful and flexible library that is widely used in the machine learning and natural language processing communities. Whether you are working on text analysis, topic modeling, or any other machine learning task, Gensim is a valuable tool to have in your toolkit.

Transformers

Transformers have become a fundamental component in the field of machine learning, particularly in natural language processing tasks. These models have revolutionized the way we approach language tasks by leveraging self-attention mechanisms to capture long-range dependencies in text data. In recent years, transformer-based models like BERT, GPT-3, and T5 have achieved state-of-the-art performance on a wide range of NLP benchmarks, showcasing the power and versatility of these architectures.

One of the key innovations of transformers is the attention mechanism, which allows the model to focus on different parts of the input sequence when making predictions. This mechanism enables transformers to capture complex relationships between words in a sentence, leading to more accurate and context-aware language models. Additionally, transformers can be easily fine-tuned on specific tasks using transfer learning, making them highly adaptable to different NLP applications.

In the realm of computer vision, transformers have also shown great promise in improving the performance of image recognition and object detection tasks. Vision transformers (ViTs) have demonstrated competitive results compared to traditional convolutional neural networks, highlighting the potential of transformers in visual data processing. By applying self-attention mechanisms to image patches, ViTs are able to effectively capture spatial relationships and semantic information in images, leading to more robust and accurate predictions.

The Complete Guide to AI Frameworks: A Comprehensive Overview

Furthermore, transformers have been successfully applied to time series analysis, where they have shown significant improvements in forecasting accuracy and signal processing tasks. By leveraging self-attention mechanisms, transformers can effectively capture temporal dependencies in sequential data, making them well-suited for time series modeling. With the ability to learn complex patterns and relationships in time series data, transformers offer a powerful tool for researchers and practitioners in the field of time series analysis.

In conclusion, transformers have emerged as a versatile and powerful tool in the machine learning landscape, with applications spanning across various domains such as NLP, computer vision, and time series analysis. By leveraging self-attention mechanisms, transformers are able to capture complex relationships in data, leading to state-of-the-art performance in a wide range of tasks. As the field of machine learning continues to evolve, transformers are expected to play a crucial role in advancing the capabilities of AI systems and pushing the boundaries of what is possible in artificial intelligence.

AllenNLP

AllenNLP, short for Allen Institute for Artificial Intelligence's Natural Language Processing, is a powerful open-source deep learning framework specifically designed for natural language processing tasks. This framework provides a wide range of tools and pre-trained models to facilitate the development of NLP applications. For people that want a comprehensive guide on NLP frameworks, AllenNLP is a must-have tool in their arsenal.

One of the key features of AllenNLP is its flexibility and modularity, which allows researchers and developers to easily customize and extend existing models for specific NLP tasks. This makes it ideal for experimenting with different architectures and algorithms, as well as for incorporating new research findings into existing models. With AllenNLP, users can quickly prototype and iterate on their NLP projects, saving time and resources in the process.

In addition to its flexibility, AllenNLP also offers a wide range of pre-trained models and datasets for common NLP tasks, such as text classification, named entity recognition, and question answering. These pre-trained models can be easily fine-tuned on new datasets or customized to suit specific requirements, making it easy for users to get started with their NLP projects without having to build models from scratch.

Furthermore, AllenNLP provides a user-friendly interface and comprehensive documentation, making it easy for users to navigate and understand the framework's capabilities. The framework also offers extensive support for distributed computing, allowing users to scale their NLP projects across multiple GPUs or even multiple machines for faster training and inference.

Overall, AllenNLP is a versatile and powerful framework for NLP tasks, offering a wide range of tools, pre-trained models, and documentation to facilitate the development of cutting-edge NLP applications. For those looking for a comprehensive guide on NLP frameworks, AllenNLP is a valuable resource that can help accelerate the development and deployment of NLP projects.

Chapter 6: Comprehensive Guide on Computer Vision Frameworks

OpenCV

OpenCV, short for Open Source Computer Vision Library, is a popular open-source computer vision and machine learning software library. It was originally developed by Intel in 1999 and has since become a widely used tool in the field of computer vision. OpenCV is designed to help developers build applications that can perform tasks such as image processing, object detection, and facial recognition.

One of the key features of OpenCV is its extensive collection of algorithms for image and video processing. These algorithms cover a wide range of tasks, including edge detection, image segmentation, object tracking, and more. OpenCV also provides tools for working with cameras, allowing developers to capture and process images and videos in real-time.

The Complete Guide to AI Frameworks: A Comprehensive Overview

In addition to its core functionality, OpenCV offers support for multiple programming languages, including C++, Python, and Java. This makes it easy for developers to integrate OpenCV into their existing projects and workflows. OpenCV is also compatible with a variety of operating systems, including Windows, macOS, and Linux, making it accessible to a wide range of users.

Another important aspect of OpenCV is its active community of developers and researchers. The OpenCV community is constantly working to improve and expand the library, adding new features and algorithms to keep pace with the latest developments in computer vision and machine learning. This vibrant community also provides support and resources for developers looking to learn more about using OpenCV in their projects.

Overall, OpenCV is an essential tool for anyone working in the field of computer vision and machine learning. Its comprehensive collection of algorithms, support for multiple programming languages, and active community make it a valuable resource for developers looking to build powerful and innovative applications in these domains. Whether you are a beginner or an experienced developer, OpenCV has something to offer for all levels of expertise.

TensorFlow Object Detection API

The TensorFlow Object Detection API is a powerful tool for creating and deploying object detection models. This subchapter will provide a comprehensive overview of how to use this API effectively for various machine learning tasks. Whether you are a beginner or an experienced practitioner, this guide will help you navigate the complexities of object detection using TensorFlow.

Object detection is a crucial task in computer vision, enabling machines to identify and locate objects within an image or video. The TensorFlow Object Detection API makes it easy to train and deploy custom object detection models, allowing you to tailor your solutions to specific use cases. By leveraging pre-trained models and fine-tuning them on your own dataset, you can achieve state-of-the-art performance with minimal effort.

The Complete Guide to AI Frameworks: A Comprehensive Overview

One of the key features of the TensorFlow Object Detection API is its support for various object detection architectures, such as Faster R-CNN, SSD, and YOLO. These architectures offer different trade-offs between speed and accuracy, allowing you to choose the best model for your specific requirements. Additionally, the API provides tools for data preprocessing, model evaluation, and visualization, making it easy to iterate on your models and improve their performance over time.

In this subchapter, we will walk you through the process of setting up the TensorFlow Object Detection API, training a custom object detection model, and deploying it for inference. We will cover best practices for data preparation, model configuration, hyperparameter tuning, and evaluation, giving you a solid foundation for building robust object detection solutions. Whether you are interested in detecting people in surveillance footage, cars on the road, or products on store shelves, this guide will help you achieve accurate and reliable results.

Overall, the TensorFlow Object Detection API is a versatile and powerful tool for tackling a wide range of object detection tasks. By following the guidance provided in this subchapter, you can harness the full potential of this API and create cutting-edge solutions for your machine learning projects. Whether you are a researcher, a developer, or a data scientist, this comprehensive guide will equip you with the knowledge and skills needed to succeed in the field of object detection using TensorFlow.

YOLO

YOLO, or "You Only Look Once," is a popular object detection algorithm that revolutionized the field of computer vision. In this subchapter, we will explore the ins and outs of YOLO and its various iterations, as well as its applications in machine learning frameworks.

The YOLO algorithm works by dividing the image into a grid and predicting bounding boxes and class probabilities for each grid cell. This results in real-time object detection with high accuracy, making it a preferred choice for tasks such as autonomous driving, surveillance, and image recognition.

The Complete Guide to AI Frameworks: A Comprehensive Overview

There are several versions of YOLO, with YOLOv3 being the most widely used. YOLOv4 and YOLOv5 have also been developed, each improving upon the previous version with increased speed and accuracy. These iterations have made YOLO a versatile and powerful tool for various machine learning tasks.

In the realm of deep learning frameworks, YOLO can be implemented using popular libraries such as TensorFlow, PyTorch, and Keras. These frameworks provide pre-trained models and easy-to-use APIs for quickly deploying YOLO in your projects.

Overall, YOLO is a game-changer in the world of computer vision and object detection. Its speed, accuracy, and real-time capabilities make it a valuable tool for a wide range of applications in machine learning frameworks. By understanding and implementing YOLO in your projects, you can take your machine learning skills to the next level.

Caffe

In the world of machine learning frameworks, one of the most popular and widely used tools is Caffe. Caffe, short for Convolutional Architecture for Fast Feature Embedding, is a deep learning framework developed by the Berkeley Vision and Learning Center. It is known for its speed and efficiency in training deep neural networks, making it a favorite among researchers and practitioners in the field.

Caffe is specifically designed for image classification and computer vision tasks, with a focus on convolutional neural networks (CNNs). Its architecture allows for easy experimentation with different network architectures and hyperparameters, making it a versatile tool for researchers looking to optimize their models. Additionally, Caffe's modular design allows for easy integration with other frameworks and libraries, making it a valuable asset in any machine learning toolkit.

One of the key features of Caffe is its speed and efficiency in training deep neural networks. Thanks to its use of GPU acceleration and optimized C++ code, Caffe can train models faster than many other deep learning frameworks. This speed is crucial for researchers and practitioners working on large-scale image recognition tasks, where training times can be a major bottleneck.

Another advantage of Caffe is its strong community support and extensive documentation. The Caffe framework has a large and active user community, with a wealth of tutorials, forums, and resources available to help users get started and troubleshoot any issues they may encounter. This level of support makes Caffe an accessible and user-friendly option for researchers and practitioners of all skill levels.

Overall, Caffe is a powerful and versatile deep learning framework that excels in image classification and computer vision tasks. Its speed, efficiency, and strong community support make it a valuable tool for researchers and practitioners looking to push the boundaries of deep learning. Whether you are new to machine learning or an experienced practitioner, Caffe is a framework worth exploring in your quest for cutting-edge AI solutions.

Dlib

Dlib is a versatile machine learning toolkit that is widely used for developing complex applications in the fields of computer vision, image processing, and deep learning. This comprehensive guide on Dlib aims to provide a detailed overview of the framework for people who are looking to expand their knowledge and skills in machine learning.

Dlib is known for its efficiency and ease of use, making it a popular choice among researchers and developers. It offers a wide range of tools and algorithms that are designed to simplify the process of building and training machine learning models. From facial recognition to object detection, Dlib provides a robust set of features that can be easily integrated into various projects.

One of the key strengths of Dlib is its support for a variety of programming languages, including C++, Python, and Java. This allows users to leverage the framework's capabilities in a language that they are most comfortable with. Additionally, Dlib is compatible with popular machine learning libraries such as TensorFlow and PyTorch, making it easy to combine different tools and resources for more advanced projects.

In addition to its wide range of functionalities, Dlib also offers comprehensive documentation and tutorials to help users get started with the framework. Whether you are a beginner or an experienced developer, Dlib provides the resources needed to learn and master the intricacies of machine learning. With its user-friendly interface and extensive support, Dlib is a valuable tool for anyone looking to delve deeper into the world of artificial intelligence.

Overall, Dlib is a powerful and versatile framework that is well-suited for a wide range of machine learning applications. Whether you are interested in computer vision, natural language processing, or deep learning, Dlib offers a comprehensive set of tools and resources to help you achieve your goals. By exploring the capabilities of Dlib and experimenting with its various features, you can gain valuable insights and skills that will enhance your understanding of machine learning.

Chapter 7: Comprehensive Guide on Transfer Learning Frameworks

TensorFlow Hub

TensorFlow Hub is a powerful library that allows users to access pre-trained machine learning models and modules for a wide range of tasks. This subchapter will provide a comprehensive overview of TensorFlow Hub, including its features, benefits, and how to effectively use it in your machine learning projects.

One of the key benefits of TensorFlow Hub is the access to a vast collection of pre-trained models and modules that can be easily integrated into your own projects. These models cover a wide range of tasks, including image classification, text processing, and more. This can save you valuable time and resources by leveraging the expertise of other developers and researchers in the field.

In addition to pre-trained models, TensorFlow Hub also provides a platform for sharing and discovering new models and modules. This collaborative aspect of the library allows users to contribute their own models and share them with the wider machine learning community. This can lead to the development of new and innovative solutions to complex problems.

The Complete Guide to AI Frameworks: A Comprehensive Overview

Another advantage of TensorFlow Hub is its ease of use and integration with other TensorFlow libraries and tools. The library is designed to be user-friendly and accessible, making it suitable for both beginners and experienced developers alike. Additionally, TensorFlow Hub is compatible with popular deep learning frameworks such as Keras, making it easy to incorporate pre-trained models into your existing projects.

Overall, TensorFlow Hub is a valuable resource for anyone working in the field of machine learning. Whether you are a researcher looking to leverage pre-trained models for your experiments, or a developer looking to enhance the capabilities of your applications, TensorFlow Hub has something to offer. By exploring the features and benefits of this library, you can unlock new possibilities for your machine learning projects and stay ahead of the curve in this rapidly evolving field.

PyTorch Hub

In recent years, PyTorch has emerged as one of the most popular and powerful deep learning frameworks in the machine learning community. With its flexibility, scalability, and ease of use, PyTorch has become a go-to tool for researchers and developers alike. One of the key features that sets PyTorch apart is PyTorch Hub, a repository of pre-trained models, datasets, and other resources that can be easily accessed and utilized in your own projects.

PyTorch Hub serves as a centralized hub for the PyTorch community, providing a wide range of pre-trained models for tasks such as image classification, object detection, text generation, and more. These models are trained on large datasets and fine-tuned for specific tasks, saving users valuable time and resources in training their own models from scratch. By simply downloading a pre-trained model from PyTorch Hub, users can quickly integrate state-of-the-art algorithms into their own projects with minimal effort.

In addition to pre-trained models, PyTorch Hub also offers a variety of datasets that can be used for training and testing machine learning models. These datasets cover a wide range of domains, including computer vision, natural language processing, and reinforcement learning. By providing easy access to high-quality datasets, PyTorch Hub enables researchers and developers to experiment with new ideas and algorithms without the need to collect and preprocess data themselves.

Furthermore, PyTorch Hub provides a platform for sharing and collaborating on machine learning projects. Users can upload their own models, datasets, and code to PyTorch Hub, making it easier for others to reproduce their results and build upon their work. This collaborative aspect of PyTorch Hub fosters a sense of community within the machine learning community, allowing researchers and developers to learn from each other and advance the field together.

Overall, PyTorch Hub is a valuable resource for anyone working in the field of machine learning. Whether you are a beginner looking to get started with deep learning or an experienced researcher looking to accelerate your projects, PyTorch Hub has something to offer. By providing easy access to pre-trained models, datasets, and a platform for sharing and collaboration, PyTorch Hub is helping to drive innovation and progress in the field of machine learning.

Keras Applications

Keras Applications are pre-trained deep learning models that can be easily utilized for a variety of tasks in machine learning and deep learning projects. These models are built using the Keras library, which is a high-level neural networks API written in Python. Keras Applications provide a convenient way for developers to leverage the power of deep learning without having to train models from scratch, saving time and resources in the process.

One of the key benefits of using Keras Applications is the wide range of pre-trained models available for different tasks, such as image classification, object detection, text generation, and more. These models have been trained on large datasets and have achieved state-of-the-art performance in their respective domains, making them ideal for transfer learning and fine-tuning on new datasets. By using Keras Applications, developers can quickly build and deploy machine learning models without the need for extensive training and optimization.

Some popular Keras Applications include VGG16, ResNet, InceptionV3, and MobileNet, which have been widely used in research and industry for various computer vision tasks. These models can be easily imported into Keras with just a few lines of code, allowing developers to focus on the specific task at hand rather than spending time on model architecture and training. Additionally, Keras Applications are compatible with popular deep learning frameworks such as TensorFlow and Theano, making it easy to integrate them into existing workflows.

In addition to image-related tasks, Keras Applications also offer models for natural language processing (NLP) tasks, such as text classification, sentiment analysis, and language translation. Models like BERT, GPT-2, and Word2Vec can be easily loaded into Keras and fine-tuned on custom datasets for specific NLP tasks. This enables developers to build powerful NLP applications with minimal effort, thanks to the rich ecosystem of pre-trained models available in Keras Applications.

Overall, Keras Applications provide a valuable resource for developers looking to leverage the power of deep learning in their projects. Whether you are working on computer vision, NLP, or other machine learning tasks, Keras Applications offer a straightforward way to incorporate pre-trained models into your workflow. By taking advantage of these models, you can accelerate the development process and achieve state-of-the-art performance in your machine learning applications.

OpenAI CLIP

The Complete Guide to AI Frameworks: A Comprehensive Overview

OpenAI CLIP, or Contrastive Language-Image Pre-training, is a cutting-edge machine learning model that has taken the AI world by storm. Developed by the renowned research lab OpenAI, CLIP is a versatile model that can understand and generate images based on natural language descriptions. This groundbreaking technology has the ability to bridge the gap between text and images, opening up a world of possibilities for applications in fields such as computer vision, natural language processing, and more.

One of the key features of OpenAI CLIP is its ability to learn from a diverse range of data sources, making it a highly adaptable and robust model. By pre-training on a large dataset of images and text captions from the internet, CLIP can effectively learn to understand the relationship between different modalities of data. This flexibility allows the model to generalize well to new tasks and datasets, making it a valuable tool for a wide range of applications.

In the realm of computer vision, OpenAI CLIP has demonstrated impressive performance on a variety of tasks, such as image classification, object detection, and image generation. By leveraging the power of natural language descriptions, CLIP can accurately interpret and generate images based on textual input, achieving state-of-the-art results on benchmark datasets. This makes the model particularly useful for tasks where labeled image data is scarce or expensive to obtain.

In the field of natural language processing, OpenAI CLIP has also shown great promise. By training on a large corpus of text data, the model can effectively understand and generate textual descriptions of images, enabling it to perform tasks such as image captioning and visual question-answering. This cross-modal understanding of text and images makes CLIP a powerful tool for applications that require multimodal data processing.

Overall, OpenAI CLIP represents a major advancement in the field of machine learning, offering a versatile and powerful model that can bridge the gap between text and images. With its impressive performance on a wide range of tasks and datasets, CLIP is poised to revolutionize the way we interact with and process multimodal data. For researchers and practitioners looking to explore the cutting edge of AI technology, OpenAI CLIP is a must-have tool in their arsenal.

Hugging Face Transformers

Hugging Face Transformers is a popular open-source library that provides state-of-the-art natural language processing (NLP) capabilities. This subchapter will delve into the various features and functionalities of Hugging Face Transformers, making it an essential read for anyone interested in harnessing the power of NLP in their machine learning projects.

One of the key strengths of Hugging Face Transformers is its extensive library of pre-trained models, which cover a wide range of NLP tasks such as sentiment analysis, text classification, and named entity recognition. These models have been fine-tuned on large datasets to achieve impressive performance on various NLP benchmarks, making them a valuable resource for developers looking to build cutting-edge NLP applications.

In addition to pre-trained models, Hugging Face Transformers also offers a user-friendly API that allows developers to easily load, fine-tune, and deploy NLP models in their own projects. The library supports popular deep learning frameworks such as PyTorch and TensorFlow, making it accessible to a wide range of developers with different preferences and skill levels.

Furthermore, Hugging Face Transformers provides a powerful set of tools for fine-tuning pre-trained models on custom datasets, enabling developers to adapt existing models to specific NLP tasks and domains. This flexibility makes it a versatile tool for building custom NLP solutions that meet the unique requirements of different applications.

Overall, Hugging Face Transformers is a comprehensive and flexible library that empowers developers to leverage the latest advancements in NLP for their machine learning projects. Whether you are a seasoned data scientist or a beginner looking to explore the world of NLP, this subchapter will provide you with the knowledge and tools you need to succeed in your NLP endeavors.

Chapter 8: Comprehensive Guide on Bayesian Machine Learning Frameworks

PyMC3

PyMC3 is a probabilistic programming framework that allows users to perform Bayesian statistical modeling in Python. It provides a flexible and intuitive way to specify probabilistic models using a high-level syntax, making it easy for users to build complex models without the need for extensive mathematical knowledge. PyMC3 is particularly well-suited for tasks such as parameter estimation, hypothesis testing, and model comparison, making it a valuable tool for researchers and practitioners in a wide range of fields.

One of the key features of PyMC3 is its support for a wide range of probabilistic distributions, including continuous, discrete, and multivariate distributions. This allows users to easily specify the likelihood and prior distributions of their models, as well as incorporate domain-specific knowledge into their analyses. PyMC3 also provides built-in support for Markov chain Monte Carlo (MCMC) sampling algorithms, which allows users to estimate the posterior distribution of their models and perform inference on the parameters of interest.

Another important feature of PyMC3 is its support for automatic differentiation using Theano, a library for numerical computation in Python. This allows users to specify complex probabilistic models using a symbolic syntax, making it easier to specify and optimize models with large numbers of parameters. PyMC3 also provides support for variational inference algorithms, which can be used to approximate the posterior distribution of a model when MCMC sampling is not feasible.

In addition to its core modeling capabilities, PyMC3 also provides a range of utilities for visualizing and diagnosing the output of Bayesian analyses. Users can easily generate trace plots, posterior distributions, and convergence diagnostics to assess the quality of their models and identify potential issues. PyMC3 also provides support for model comparison using techniques such as Bayesian model averaging and hypothesis testing, allowing users to evaluate the relative performance of different models and make informed decisions based on their data.

Overall, PyMC3 is a powerful and flexible framework for performing Bayesian statistical modeling in Python. Its intuitive syntax, support for a wide range of probabilistic distributions, and built-in support for advanced inference algorithms make it a valuable tool for researchers and practitioners in a wide range of fields. Whether you are new to Bayesian modeling or an experienced practitioner, PyMC3 provides a comprehensive and user-friendly environment for building and evaluating complex probabilistic models.

Edward

Edward is a versatile probabilistic programming framework that is designed to be flexible and easy to use. It is built on top of TensorFlow, allowing users to easily combine the power of deep learning with probabilistic modeling. Edward provides a wide range of probabilistic models, inference algorithms, and evaluation tools, making it a comprehensive solution for a variety of machine learning tasks.

One of the key features of Edward is its support for Bayesian machine learning, which allows users to specify complex probabilistic models and perform efficient inference using a variety of algorithms. This makes it ideal for tasks such as uncertainty estimation, anomaly detection, and decision making under uncertainty. Edward also supports variational inference, Monte Carlo methods, and Hamiltonian Monte Carlo, giving users the flexibility to choose the best approach for their specific problem.

In addition to Bayesian machine learning, Edward also offers support for generative adversarial networks (GANs), a powerful approach to training generative models. GANs have been successfully applied to tasks such as image generation, style transfer, and data augmentation. With Edward, users can easily build and train GAN models, making it a valuable tool for researchers and practitioners working in the field of deep learning.

Another important feature of Edward is its support for autoML, which aims to automate the process of building and optimizing machine learning models. This can help users save time and resources, while also improving the performance of their models. Edward provides a wide range of autoML tools, including automated feature engineering, hyperparameter optimization, and model selection, making it a comprehensive solution for automated machine learning.

The Complete Guide to AI Frameworks: A Comprehensive Overview

Overall, Edward is a powerful and flexible machine learning framework that offers a wide range of tools and algorithms for building and training probabilistic models. Whether you are working on Bayesian machine learning, deep learning, generative modeling, or autoML, Edward provides the tools you need to tackle complex machine learning tasks. With its ease of use and comprehensive features, Edward is a valuable resource for researchers, data scientists, and machine learning enthusiasts alike.

Stan

In the world of machine learning frameworks, one name that stands out is Stan. Stan is a popular probabilistic programming language used for statistical modeling and data analysis. It is known for its flexibility, scalability, and efficiency in handling complex models. In this subchapter, we will delve into the details of Stan and explore its features, applications, and benefits for machine learning enthusiasts.

Stan is widely used in the field of Bayesian machine learning, where it excels in handling complex hierarchical models and inference algorithms. It is based on a cutting-edge algorithm called Hamiltonian Monte Carlo (HMC), which allows for efficient sampling from high-dimensional posterior distributions. This makes Stan an ideal choice for researchers and data scientists working on challenging problems in statistics, machine learning, and computational biology.

One of the key strengths of Stan is its ability to seamlessly integrate with other machine learning frameworks and tools. It provides interfaces for popular programming languages such as R, Python, and Julia, allowing users to leverage their existing code and libraries. This interoperability makes Stan a versatile choice for building and deploying machine learning models across different platforms and environments.

In addition to its capabilities in Bayesian machine learning, Stan is also used in a wide range of applications, including natural language processing, computer vision, and time series analysis. Its rich set of features, including automatic differentiation, probabilistic modeling, and Markov chain Monte Carlo (MCMC) sampling, make it a powerful tool for solving diverse problems in machine learning and data science.

The Complete Guide to AI Frameworks: A Comprehensive Overview

Whether you are a beginner looking to learn the basics of machine learning frameworks or an experienced practitioner seeking advanced techniques, Stan has something to offer for everyone. By mastering Stan, you can unlock new possibilities in your machine learning projects and gain a deeper understanding of complex probabilistic models. So, dive into the world of Stan and explore the endless possibilities it offers for your machine learning journey.

Pyro

Pyro is a probabilistic programming framework that is built on top of PyTorch, making it a powerful tool for building Bayesian models. In this subchapter, we will explore the key features of Pyro and how it can be used in machine learning applications.

One of the main advantages of using Pyro is its flexibility in modeling complex probabilistic systems. With Pyro, users can define probabilistic models using simple Python code, allowing for easy experimentation and iteration. This makes it ideal for researchers and practitioners who need to quickly prototype and test different models.

Pyro also provides a rich set of inference algorithms, including variational inference and Markov Chain Monte Carlo (MCMC) methods. These algorithms allow users to estimate the parameters of their models and make predictions based on observed data. Additionally, Pyro supports parallel computation, making it possible to scale up to large datasets and complex models.

Another key feature of Pyro is its integration with PyTorch, a popular deep learning framework. This allows users to combine probabilistic modeling with deep learning, enabling the development of models that can capture complex patterns in data. By leveraging the strengths of both frameworks, users can build more robust and accurate machine learning models.

Overall, Pyro is a powerful and flexible framework for building probabilistic models in machine learning. Its integration with PyTorch, support for various inference algorithms, and scalability make it a valuable tool for researchers and practitioners working in areas such as Bayesian machine learning, generative modeling, and reinforcement learning. With Pyro, users can unlock new possibilities in their machine learning projects and push the boundaries of what is possible in the field.

TFP

TFP, or TensorFlow Probability, is a powerful framework that combines the capabilities of TensorFlow with probabilistic modeling. This framework is designed for researchers and practitioners who want to incorporate uncertainty into their machine learning models. TFP provides a wide range of tools for building probabilistic models, including probabilistic layers, distributions, and inference algorithms.

One of the key features of TFP is its ability to perform Bayesian inference, which allows users to quantify uncertainty in their models and make more informed decisions. Bayesian inference is particularly useful in scenarios where data is limited or noisy, as it can help to account for uncertainty in the model's predictions. TFP also provides tools for model evaluation, including metrics for assessing the quality of probabilistic models and methods for comparing different models.

In addition to Bayesian inference, TFP also offers support for deep probabilistic models, which combine the representational power of deep learning with the flexibility of probabilistic modeling. These models can be used for a wide range of tasks, including regression, classification, and generative modeling. TFP provides a variety of pre-built probabilistic layers that can be easily integrated into deep learning models, making it easy to experiment with different architectures.

Another key feature of TFP is its support for probabilistic programming, which allows users to define complex probabilistic models using a high-level programming language. This makes it easy to express a wide range of probabilistic models, from simple linear regression models to complex hierarchical models. TFP also provides tools for performing inference on these models, including variational inference and Markov chain Monte Carlo (MCMC) methods.

Overall, TFP is a comprehensive framework for building and training probabilistic models. Whether you are interested in Bayesian inference, deep probabilistic models, or probabilistic programming, TFP provides the tools and resources you need to explore the world of probabilistic machine learning. With TFP, you can take your machine learning models to the next level by incorporating uncertainty and making more informed decisions.

Chapter 9: Comprehensive Guide on Generative Adversarial Networks (GANs) Frameworks

TensorFlow-GAN

TensorFlow-GAN, short for TensorFlow Generative Adversarial Networks, is a powerful framework for creating and training GANs, a type of deep learning model that consists of two neural networks – a generator and a discriminator – that work together to generate realistic data. This subchapter will provide a comprehensive overview of TensorFlow-GAN, including its features, benefits, and how to get started using it.

One of the key features of TensorFlow-GAN is its ease of use and flexibility. With TensorFlow-GAN, users can easily define and train GAN models using high-level APIs, making it ideal for both beginners and experienced machine learning practitioners. Additionally, TensorFlow-GAN provides a wide range of pre-built models and tools, allowing users to quickly get started with their GAN projects without having to build everything from scratch.

Another advantage of TensorFlow-GAN is its performance and scalability. The framework is built on top of TensorFlow, a popular open-source deep learning library developed by Google, which means it can take advantage of TensorFlow's efficient computation and distributed training capabilities. This makes TensorFlow-GAN suitable for training large-scale GAN models on large datasets, making it a valuable tool for researchers and developers working on complex generative modeling tasks.

In addition to its ease of use and performance, TensorFlow-GAN also offers a variety of pre-trained models and tutorials that can help users get started with their GAN projects quickly. These resources cover a wide range of applications, from image generation to text generation, and provide step-by-step guidance on how to train and evaluate GAN models using TensorFlow-GAN.

Overall, TensorFlow-GAN is a comprehensive and powerful framework for creating and training GAN models. Whether you are a beginner looking to get started with generative modeling or an experienced practitioner working on advanced research projects, TensorFlow-GAN has the tools and resources you need to succeed. With its ease of use, performance, and scalability, TensorFlow-GAN is a valuable addition to any machine learning practitioner's toolkit.

PyTorch-GAN

In the world of machine learning, Generative Adversarial Networks (GANs) have gained significant attention for their ability to generate realistic data samples. PyTorch, a popular deep learning framework, has also been widely adopted for its flexibility and ease of use. In this subchapter, we will delve into PyTorch-GAN, a combination of PyTorch and GANs that allows users to create powerful generative models.

PyTorch-GAN provides a framework for training GAN models using PyTorch's extensive library of neural network modules and optimization algorithms. With PyTorch-GAN, users can easily define and train GAN architectures for various applications such as image generation, text generation, and more. The flexibility of PyTorch allows for easy experimentation with different GAN architectures and training techniques, making it a popular choice among researchers and practitioners.

The Complete Guide to AI Frameworks: A Comprehensive Overview

One of the key features of PyTorch-GAN is its support for custom loss functions and training procedures. This allows users to tailor the training process to their specific needs and objectives, enabling them to achieve better results with their GAN models. Additionally, PyTorch-GAN provides pre-trained models and utilities for common tasks, making it easy for users to get started with GANs without having to build everything from scratch.

PyTorch-GAN also offers a range of evaluation metrics and visualization tools to help users assess the performance of their GAN models. These tools allow users to analyze the quality of generated samples, measure the diversity of generated outputs, and compare different GAN architectures. By providing these insights, PyTorch-GAN empowers users to iterate on their models and improve their performance over time.

In conclusion, PyTorch-GAN is a powerful tool for creating and training GAN models using the PyTorch framework. Its flexibility, ease of use, and support for custom loss functions make it a valuable resource for researchers and practitioners working on generative modeling tasks. Whether you are new to GANs or an experienced practitioner, PyTorch-GAN offers a comprehensive and user-friendly environment for exploring the potential of generative adversarial networks.

Keras-GAN

Keras-GAN is a subchapter in "The Complete Guide to Machine Learning Frameworks: A Comprehensive Overview" that is designed for people who want a comprehensive guide to various machine learning frameworks, including deep learning, reinforcement learning, natural language processing, computer vision, transfer learning, Bayesian machine learning, Generative Adversarial Networks (GANs), AutoML, Federated Learning, and Time Series Analysis. In this section, we will delve into the details of Keras-GAN, which is a popular framework for implementing GANs.

The Complete Guide to AI Frameworks: A Comprehensive Overview

Generative Adversarial Networks (GANs) have gained significant attention in the machine learning community due to their ability to generate realistic data. Keras-GAN is a high-level neural networks API that is built on top of TensorFlow and provides a user-friendly interface for creating and training GANs. With Keras-GAN, developers can easily build and train GAN models for various applications, such as image generation, style transfer, and data augmentation.

One of the key features of Keras-GAN is its modular design, which allows users to easily customize and extend the functionality of GAN models. This makes it suitable for researchers and developers who want to experiment with different architectures and loss functions. Additionally, Keras-GAN provides pre-built components for common GAN architectures, such as DCGAN, WGAN, and CycleGAN, making it easy for users to get started with their projects.

In addition to its modular design, Keras-GAN also offers a range of utility functions for data preprocessing, evaluation, and visualization. These functions help users streamline the development process and enable them to focus on the core aspects of their GAN models. Furthermore, Keras-GAN provides comprehensive documentation and tutorials that guide users through the implementation and training of GAN models, making it accessible to both beginners and experienced users.

Overall, Keras-GAN is a powerful and versatile framework for building and training GAN models. Its user-friendly interface, modular design, and extensive documentation make it an ideal choice for researchers, developers, and machine learning enthusiasts who want to explore the capabilities of GANs. Whether you are interested in image generation, style transfer, or data augmentation, Keras-GAN provides the tools and resources you need to bring your GAN projects to life.

DCGAN

DCGAN, or Deep Convolutional Generative Adversarial Networks, is a type of generative model that has revolutionized the field of machine learning. In this subchapter, we will delve deep into the workings of DCGANs and explore how they are used to generate realistic images.

At the core of DCGANs are two neural networks - a generator and a discriminator. The generator takes random noise as input and generates images, while the discriminator tries to distinguish between real images and fake images generated by the generator. Through this adversarial training process, the generator learns to create images that are indistinguishable from real images.

One of the key features of DCGANs is their ability to generate high-quality images with sharp details and realistic textures. This is achieved through the use of convolutional layers in both the generator and discriminator, which allow the networks to capture spatial dependencies in the data and generate images that are visually appealing.

DCGANs have been used in a wide range of applications, including image generation, image inpainting, and image super-resolution. They have also been used to generate synthetic data for training machine learning models in scenarios where real data is scarce or expensive to collect.

In conclusion, DCGANs are a powerful tool in the field of machine learning, enabling researchers and practitioners to generate realistic images and explore the potential of generative models. By understanding the inner workings of DCGANs and their applications, you can unlock new possibilities in your own machine learning projects.

CycleGAN

CycleGAN is a powerful deep learning framework that has gained popularity in the field of computer vision and image-to-image translation tasks. This framework is based on the generative adversarial network (GAN) architecture, which consists of two neural networks - a generator and a discriminator - that work together to generate realistic images from input images.

One of the key features of CycleGAN is its ability to learn mappings between two different domains without the need for paired training data. This is achieved through the use of cycle consistency, where the framework enforces that the transformation from one domain to the other and back should result in the original input image. This helps in preserving the content of the input image while changing its style or appearance.

CycleGAN has been successfully applied to a wide range of tasks, including style transfer, object transfiguration, and image colorization. It has also been used in applications such as artistic image synthesis, domain adaptation, and image-to-image translation. The framework has shown impressive results in generating realistic and high-quality images, making it a valuable tool for various computer vision tasks.

One of the advantages of CycleGAN is its flexibility and ease of use. The framework can be easily trained on new datasets with minimal modifications, making it suitable for a wide range of applications. Additionally, CycleGAN is open-source and has a vibrant community of developers and researchers who are constantly improving and extending its capabilities.

In conclusion, CycleGAN is a versatile and powerful deep learning framework that is widely used in the field of computer vision. Its ability to learn mappings between different domains without paired training data, coupled with its flexibility and ease of use, make it a valuable tool for researchers and developers working on image-to-image translation tasks. With its impressive results and wide range of applications, CycleGAN is a framework that is worth exploring for anyone interested in the field of machine learning and computer vision.

Chapter 10: Comprehensive Guide on AutoML Frameworks

Google Cloud AutoML

Google Cloud AutoML is a cutting-edge technology that allows users to easily build and deploy machine learning models without the need for extensive coding or machine learning expertise. This platform is designed for people who want to harness the power of machine learning in their projects, but may not have the technical background to do so using traditional methods.

One of the key features of Google Cloud AutoML is its user-friendly interface, which guides users through the process of creating and training their own machine learning models. This interface allows users to upload their own data, select the type of model they want to build, and then automatically trains the model using Google's powerful infrastructure. This streamlined process makes it easy for even beginners to get started with machine learning.

Another advantage of Google Cloud AutoML is its ability to automatically optimize and fine-tune models for specific tasks. This means that users can quickly generate high-quality models without the need for extensive manual tuning. This feature is especially useful for users who may not have the time or expertise to fine-tune models themselves.

Furthermore, Google Cloud AutoML offers a range of pre-trained models for common machine learning tasks, such as image classification and natural language processing. These pre-trained models can be easily customized and adapted to suit specific use cases, making it easy for users to get started with machine learning without having to start from scratch.

Overall, Google Cloud AutoML is a powerful tool for anyone looking to incorporate machine learning into their projects. Whether you're a beginner looking to get started with machine learning or an experienced data scientist looking to streamline your workflow, Google Cloud AutoML offers a comprehensive solution for building and deploying machine learning models with ease.

H2O.ai

H2O.ai is a popular open-source machine learning platform that is known for its ease of use and scalability. In this subchapter, we will delve deeper into the features and capabilities of H2O.ai and how it can benefit those looking to harness the power of machine learning in their projects.

The Complete Guide to AI Frameworks: A Comprehensive Overview

One of the key advantages of H2O.ai is its ability to handle large datasets with ease. Whether you are working with structured data, unstructured data, or a combination of both, H2O.ai can efficiently process and analyze the information to extract valuable insights. This makes it an ideal choice for organizations dealing with massive amounts of data in industries such as finance, healthcare, and retail.

Another standout feature of H2O.ai is its extensive library of machine learning algorithms. From traditional algorithms like linear regression and decision trees to more advanced techniques like deep learning and ensemble methods, H2O.ai offers a wide range of options to suit different use cases and data types. This flexibility allows users to experiment with different algorithms and find the ones that yield the best results for their specific tasks.

In addition to its robust algorithms, H2O.ai also provides powerful tools for model training and evaluation. Users can easily build, train, and deploy machine learning models using the platform's intuitive interface and visualization tools. Furthermore, H2O.ai includes features for hyperparameter tuning, model interpretation, and model deployment, making it a comprehensive solution for all stages of the machine learning workflow.

Overall, H2O.ai is a valuable tool for anyone looking to dive into the world of machine learning. Whether you are a seasoned data scientist or a beginner looking to get started, H2O.ai offers a user-friendly platform with powerful features and capabilities. By incorporating H2O.ai into your machine learning projects, you can leverage its advanced algorithms and tools to unlock new insights and drive innovation in your organization.

Auto-Keras

Auto-Keras is an open-source AutoML framework written in Python that allows users to automatically search for the best neural network architecture and hyperparameters for their machine learning tasks. It is designed to simplify the process of building and training deep learning models by automating the tedious tasks of hyperparameter tuning and neural network design. For people that want a comprehensive guide on AutoML frameworks, Auto-Keras is a great tool to explore.

One of the key features of Auto-Keras is its user-friendly interface, which allows users to define their machine learning problem and let the framework handle the rest. This makes it easy for beginners to get started with deep learning without having to worry about the technical details of model design and tuning. With Auto-Keras, users can quickly build and train high-quality deep learning models without the need for extensive programming knowledge.

Auto-Keras leverages neural architecture search algorithms to automatically explore the space of possible neural network architectures and hyperparameters, searching for the best combination that maximizes performance on a given dataset. This approach can save users a significant amount of time and effort compared to manual hyperparameter tuning and model selection. By using Auto-Keras, users can focus on the higher-level aspects of their machine learning tasks, such as data preprocessing and feature engineering, while the framework handles the nitty-gritty details of model design.

In addition to its automated model search capabilities, Auto-Keras also provides a range of pre-built neural network architectures that users can easily customize and fine-tune for their specific tasks. This makes it easy to experiment with different types of deep learning models and explore the performance trade-offs between simplicity and complexity. Auto-Keras also supports a wide range of machine learning tasks, including classification, regression, and image recognition, making it a versatile tool for a variety of applications.

Overall, Auto-Keras is a powerful AutoML framework that can help users streamline the process of building and training deep learning models. Whether you are a beginner looking to get started with deep learning or an experienced data scientist looking to automate the model selection process, Auto-Keras offers a comprehensive set of tools and features to meet your needs. By leveraging the power of Auto-Keras, users can accelerate their machine learning workflows and unlock new possibilities for innovation and discovery in the field of artificial intelligence.

DataRobot

The Complete Guide to AI Frameworks: A Comprehensive Overview

DataRobot is a powerful automated machine learning platform that is designed to help organizations streamline the process of building and deploying machine learning models. With DataRobot, users can quickly and easily build, test, and deploy machine learning models without the need for extensive programming knowledge or expertise. This makes it an ideal tool for organizations looking to leverage the power of machine learning without the need for a team of data scientists.

One of the key features of DataRobot is its automated model building capabilities. The platform uses advanced algorithms and machine learning techniques to analyze data and build predictive models that can be used to make informed business decisions. Users simply upload their data to the platform, select the target variable they want to predict, and let DataRobot do the rest. The platform will automatically test multiple algorithms and model configurations to find the best performing model for the given data set.

In addition to its automated model building capabilities, DataRobot also offers a range of tools and features to help users interpret and visualize their data. The platform provides interactive data visualizations, model performance metrics, and feature importance rankings to help users understand how their models are performing and make informed decisions about how to improve them. This makes it easy for users to track the performance of their models over time and make adjustments as needed.

DataRobot is also designed to be highly scalable, making it ideal for organizations with large and complex data sets. The platform can handle massive amounts of data and can build and deploy models quickly and efficiently. This makes it an ideal tool for organizations looking to leverage the power of machine learning to drive business insights and make informed decisions.

Overall, DataRobot is a comprehensive and powerful machine learning platform that is designed to help organizations of all sizes build and deploy machine learning models quickly and efficiently. Whether you are new to machine learning or an experienced data scientist, DataRobot offers a range of tools and features to help you build and deploy models that drive business insights and help you make informed decisions.

TPOT

In the world of machine learning frameworks, TPOT (Tree-based Pipeline Optimization Tool) stands out as a powerful and versatile tool for automating the process of model selection and hyperparameter optimization. Developed by researchers at the University of Pennsylvania, TPOT is designed to help data scientists and machine learning practitioners quickly build highly optimized machine learning pipelines without the need for manual intervention.

One of the key features of TPOT is its ability to search through a wide range of machine learning algorithms and hyperparameters to find the best combination for a given dataset. This automated approach can save practitioners countless hours of trial and error, allowing them to focus on interpreting and acting on the results of their models rather than getting bogged down in the minutiae of model tuning.

TPOT is particularly well-suited for tasks such as classification, regression, and clustering, making it a valuable tool for a wide range of machine learning applications. Its flexibility and ease of use make it an ideal choice for both beginners looking to get started with machine learning and experienced practitioners looking to streamline their workflow and improve the performance of their models.

In addition to its robust optimization capabilities, TPOT also provides users with detailed insights into the performance of their models, including metrics such as accuracy, precision, recall, and F1 score. This level of transparency can help practitioners understand the strengths and weaknesses of their models and make informed decisions about how to improve them.

Overall, TPOT is a valuable addition to the toolkit of any data scientist or machine learning practitioner looking to streamline their workflow and build highly optimized machine learning pipelines. By automating the process of model selection and hyperparameter optimization, TPOT can help practitioners save time, improve the performance of their models, and gain valuable insights into the strengths and weaknesses of their machine learning pipelines.

Chapter 11: Comprehensive Guide on Federated Learning Frameworks

TensorFlow Federated

TensorFlow Federated is a cutting-edge framework that allows for machine learning models to be trained on decentralized data sources. This means that instead of having all data centralized in one location, TensorFlow Federated enables models to be trained on data that is spread out across multiple devices or servers. This is particularly useful in scenarios where data privacy is a concern, as it allows for training models without having to share sensitive data.

One of the key features of TensorFlow Federated is its ability to handle federated learning, which is a machine learning approach that allows for models to be trained on data that is stored locally on individual devices. This is especially beneficial in healthcare applications, where patient data is highly sensitive and needs to be kept private. TensorFlow Federated enables models to be trained on this data without compromising patient privacy, making it a valuable tool for healthcare professionals looking to leverage machine learning for medical research.

Another advantage of TensorFlow Federated is its scalability. By allowing models to be trained on decentralized data sources, TensorFlow Federated can easily handle large datasets that would be impractical to centralize. This makes it a popular choice for organizations working with big data, as it enables them to train models on vast amounts of information without having to worry about the limitations of centralized storage.

In addition to its privacy and scalability benefits, TensorFlow Federated also offers a high level of customization. Users can tailor their models to suit their specific needs, whether they are working on natural language processing, computer vision, or any other machine learning task. This flexibility makes TensorFlow Federated a versatile tool that can be adapted to a wide range of applications, making it a valuable resource for machine learning practitioners across various industries.

Overall, TensorFlow Federated is a powerful framework that is revolutionizing the field of machine learning. Its ability to handle federated learning, scalability, and customization make it a valuable tool for organizations looking to leverage decentralized data sources for training machine learning models. Whether you are working on healthcare applications, big data analysis, or any other machine learning task, TensorFlow Federated is a comprehensive solution that can meet your needs and help you achieve your goals in the field of machine learning.

PySyft

PySyft is an open-source framework that enables secure, privacy-preserving machine learning. It is designed to facilitate decentralized and federated learning, allowing machine learning models to be trained across multiple devices without compromising data privacy. PySyft integrates seamlessly with popular deep learning frameworks such as PyTorch and TensorFlow, making it a versatile tool for researchers and developers alike.

One of the key features of PySyft is its support for differential privacy, a technique that adds noise to the training data to prevent the leakage of sensitive information. This ensures that individual data points cannot be reverse-engineered from the model, protecting the privacy of users in decentralized learning environments. PySyft also includes tools for secure multi-party computation, enabling multiple parties to collaborate on training models without revealing their private data to each other.

In addition to its privacy-preserving capabilities, PySyft offers a range of tools for collaborative machine learning. These include tools for federated learning, where models are trained across multiple devices, as well as tools for secure aggregation of model updates. This makes PySyft well-suited for applications in healthcare, finance, and other industries where data privacy is of utmost importance.

PySyft is actively maintained by a community of developers and researchers, ensuring that the framework remains up-to-date with the latest advancements in machine learning and privacy-preserving technologies. The framework is also well-documented, with tutorials and examples to help users get started with their own projects. Whether you are interested in federated learning, secure multi-party computation, or differential privacy, PySyft provides a comprehensive set of tools for building privacy-preserving machine learning models.

Overall, PySyft is a powerful framework for researchers and developers looking to build privacy-preserving machine learning models. Its support for federated learning, secure multi-party computation, and differential privacy make it a valuable tool for a wide range of applications. If you are interested in exploring decentralized and privacy-preserving machine learning, PySyft is definitely worth checking out.

Flower

In the world of machine learning frameworks, the concept of a "flower" may seem out of place. However, just like a flower blossoms and grows with care and attention, machine learning frameworks also require nurturing and understanding to reach their full potential. In this subchapter, we will explore the various aspects of machine learning frameworks that can be likened to the delicate beauty of a flower.

First and foremost, a machine learning framework can be thought of as the stem of a flower – providing structure and support for the algorithms and models that will be built upon it. Just as a stem delivers nutrients and water to help a flower thrive, a well-designed framework will offer the necessary tools and resources for developers to create powerful machine learning solutions.

Next, we can compare the algorithms used within a framework to the petals of a flower – each one unique and essential to the overall beauty and functionality of the system. Just as a flower's petals work together to attract pollinators and ensure reproduction, machine learning algorithms collaborate to analyze data, make predictions, and optimize performance.

The roots of a flower are crucial for anchoring it in the soil and absorbing nutrients from the environment. In the same way, the underlying architecture of a machine learning framework provides the foundation for building and training models. Understanding the roots of a framework – such as its computational graph structure or optimization techniques – is essential for maximizing its capabilities.

As a flower blooms and reaches its full potential, so too can a machine learning framework evolve and improve over time. By staying up-to-date with the latest advancements in the field, developers can ensure that their frameworks are constantly growing and adapting to new challenges. Just as a flower must be pruned and cared for to thrive, machine learning frameworks require ongoing maintenance and optimization to remain effective.

In conclusion, the analogy of a flower can help us better understand the intricate and interconnected nature of machine learning frameworks. By nurturing these frameworks with care and attention, developers can harness their full potential and create innovative solutions that blossom and flourish in the ever-changing landscape of technology.

IBM Federated Learning

In recent years, Federated Learning has emerged as a promising approach to machine learning that allows multiple parties to collaboratively build a shared model without sharing their raw data. IBM, a leader in technology and innovation, has been at the forefront of developing Federated Learning frameworks that enable secure and privacy-preserving collaboration among multiple stakeholders.

IBM Federated Learning is a distributed machine learning approach that allows organizations to train models across multiple devices or servers while keeping data localized. This decentralized approach not only ensures data privacy and security but also enables efficient model training on edge devices with limited computational resources.

One of the key advantages of IBM Federated Learning is its ability to scale across geographically distributed devices and servers, making it ideal for organizations with a global footprint. By leveraging the power of edge computing, IBM Federated Learning enables real-time model training and inference on devices such as smartphones, IoT devices, and edge servers.

IBM Federated Learning also provides built-in mechanisms for data encryption, differential privacy, and model aggregation, ensuring that sensitive information remains protected throughout the training process. This level of security and privacy protection is crucial for organizations operating in highly regulated industries such as healthcare, finance, and telecommunications.

Overall, IBM Federated Learning is a powerful tool for organizations looking to harness the collective intelligence of their data without compromising privacy or security. By leveraging the capabilities of IBM Federated Learning, businesses can accelerate their machine learning initiatives and drive innovation in a secure and collaborative manner.

OpenMined

OpenMined is a revolutionary open-source community that is focused on privacy-preserving, decentralized technologies. The community believes in the power of collaboration and aims to build tools and frameworks that enable secure and privacy-focused machine learning applications. OpenMined is at the forefront of the movement towards democratizing AI and ensuring that individuals have control over their own data.

One of the key principles of OpenMined is the concept of "privacy by design". This means that privacy and security considerations are built into the design of their tools and frameworks from the very beginning. This ensures that data remains secure and private throughout the machine learning process, from data collection to model training and deployment.

OpenMined provides a wide range of tools and frameworks that are designed to make it easy for developers to build privacy-preserving machine learning applications. These tools include PySyft, a Python library for secure multi-party computation, and TenSEAL, a library for homomorphic encryption. By using these tools, developers can ensure that sensitive data remains encrypted and secure, even when shared with multiple parties for collaborative machine learning projects.

In addition to providing tools and frameworks, OpenMined also offers educational resources and tutorials to help developers learn how to build privacy-preserving machine learning applications. The community is committed to making privacy-preserving AI accessible to everyone, regardless of their background or level of expertise. By joining the OpenMined community, developers can collaborate with like-minded individuals and contribute to the advancement of privacy-preserving technologies.

Overall, OpenMined is a game-changer in the field of machine learning frameworks. By prioritizing privacy and security, the community is paving the way for a more ethical and responsible approach to AI development. For anyone looking to learn more about privacy-preserving machine learning frameworks, OpenMined is definitely a community worth exploring.

Chapter 12: Comprehensive Guide on Time Series Analysis Frameworks

Prophet

In the realm of machine learning frameworks, the Prophet framework stands out as a powerful tool for time series forecasting. Developed by Facebook, Prophet is designed to handle time series data with strong seasonal patterns and multiple trends. For people that want a comprehensive guide on time series analysis frameworks, Prophet is a must-have in their toolkit.

One of the key features of Prophet is its ability to automatically detect and model seasonality in the data. This makes it particularly well-suited for forecasting tasks where seasonality plays a significant role, such as retail sales, demand forecasting, and weather predictions. Additionally, Prophet allows users to specify custom seasonality patterns, making it flexible and adaptable to a wide range of time series data.

Prophet also incorporates a robust trend modeling component, which can capture both short-term fluctuations and long-term trends in the data. This makes it ideal for forecasting scenarios where the underlying patterns may be complex and changing over time. With Prophet, users can easily visualize and interpret the trends in their data, helping them make more informed decisions based on the forecasted outcomes.

Another advantage of Prophet is its ability to handle missing data and outliers gracefully. The framework is designed to handle data with irregularities and data gaps, ensuring that users can still make accurate forecasts even in the presence of incomplete or noisy data. This feature sets Prophet apart from other time series forecasting tools, making it a reliable choice for real-world applications.

Overall, Prophet is a comprehensive and user-friendly framework that is well-suited for a wide range of time series forecasting tasks. Whether you are a seasoned data scientist or a beginner in the field of machine learning, Prophet offers a powerful set of tools and features to help you analyze and forecast time series data with confidence. For people that want a comprehensive guide on time series analysis frameworks, Prophet is a valuable asset that can help them unlock the potential of their time series data.

Statsmodels

Statsmodels is a powerful Python library that provides a wide range of tools for statistical analysis. It is particularly useful for conducting regression analysis, time series analysis, and hypothesis testing. In this subchapter, we will explore the key features of Statsmodels and how it can be used in various machine learning applications.

One of the main strengths of Statsmodels is its comprehensive support for linear regression models. Whether you are interested in simple linear regression or more complex multiple regression models, Statsmodels provides a user-friendly interface for fitting and interpreting these models. Additionally, Statsmodels offers a variety of diagnostic tools for evaluating the quality of regression models, such as residual analysis and goodness-of-fit tests.

In addition to linear regression, Statsmodels also supports a range of other statistical models, including generalized linear models, time series models, and mixed effects models. This makes it a versatile tool for a wide range of statistical analyses, from simple hypothesis testing to more advanced predictive modeling. By leveraging the capabilities of Statsmodels, data scientists and researchers can gain valuable insights from their data and make informed decisions.

Another key feature of Statsmodels is its integration with other Python libraries, such as NumPy and pandas. This allows users to easily manipulate and analyze data before fitting statistical models, streamlining the data preprocessing and modeling process. Statsmodels also provides extensive documentation and examples, making it easy for users to get started with the library and explore its capabilities.

Overall, Statsmodels is a valuable tool for anyone working in the field of machine learning and statistics. Whether you are a beginner looking to learn the basics of statistical modeling or an experienced data scientist looking for a flexible and powerful tool for complex analyses, Statsmodels has something to offer. By incorporating Statsmodels into your workflow, you can enhance your analytical capabilities and make more informed decisions based on data-driven insights.

ARIMA

For people that want a comprehensive guide on Time Series Analysis Frameworks, one of the most important tools to consider is ARIMA. ARIMA, which stands for Autoregressive Integrated Moving Average, is a popular statistical method used for analyzing and forecasting time series data. It is a versatile model that can capture the complex patterns and trends present in time series data, making it a valuable tool for a wide range of applications.

The Complete Guide to AI Frameworks: A Comprehensive Overview

ARIMA models are made up of three components: autoregressive (AR), differencing (I), and moving average (MA). The autoregressive component accounts for the relationship between an observation and a certain number of lagged observations. The differencing component is used to make the time series stationary, while the moving average component captures the relationship between an observation and the residual errors from a moving average model.

One of the key advantages of using ARIMA models is their ability to handle non-stationary time series data. By differencing the data, ARIMA models can remove trends and seasonality, making the data suitable for analysis. This makes ARIMA a powerful tool for forecasting future values based on past observations, making it a valuable tool for businesses and researchers looking to make data-driven decisions.

In order to build an ARIMA model, it is important to select the appropriate values for the AR, I, and MA components. This process, known as model selection, can be done using techniques such as the Akaike Information Criterion (AIC) or the Bayesian Information Criterion (BIC). These criteria help determine the best-fitting model for the data, ensuring accurate forecasts and reliable results.

Overall, ARIMA is a valuable tool for analyzing and forecasting time series data. Whether you are working with financial data, stock prices, or weather patterns, ARIMA can help you uncover valuable insights and make informed decisions. By understanding the components of ARIMA and how to select the best model for your data, you can harness the power of this versatile framework for your own time series analysis needs.

LSTM

LSTM, or Long Short-Term Memory, is a type of recurrent neural network architecture that is particularly well-suited for processing and making predictions on sequences of data. In the world of machine learning frameworks, LSTM has become a popular choice for tasks such as speech recognition, language translation, and time series forecasting. In this subchapter, we will delve into the inner workings of LSTM and explore its applications in various domains.

One of the key features of LSTM is its ability to effectively capture long-term dependencies in sequential data. Traditional recurrent neural networks have difficulties in learning and retaining information over long sequences, leading to issues such as vanishing or exploding gradients. LSTM addresses this problem by introducing a memory cell that can store information over long periods of time, allowing the network to remember important patterns and make accurate predictions.

In the realm of deep learning frameworks, LSTM is often implemented using libraries such as TensorFlow, PyTorch, and Keras. These frameworks provide developers with high-level APIs for building and training LSTM models, making it easier to experiment with different architectures and hyperparameters. By leveraging these tools, researchers and practitioners can quickly prototype and deploy LSTM-based solutions for a wide range of applications.

In the field of natural language processing, LSTM has proven to be particularly effective for tasks such as sentiment analysis, named entity recognition, and language modeling. Its ability to learn complex patterns in textual data has made it a popular choice for developing state-of-the-art language models and chatbots. By fine-tuning pre-trained LSTM models on specific datasets, researchers can achieve impressive results in various NLP tasks.

Overall, LSTM is a powerful tool in the machine learning practitioner's arsenal, offering a flexible and efficient way to model sequential data. Whether you are working on time series analysis, language processing, or any other domain that involves sequential data, understanding LSTM and its applications can greatly enhance your modeling capabilities. In the following chapters, we will explore more advanced topics related to LSTM and delve into cutting-edge research in the field of deep learning frameworks.

XGBoost

XGBoost, short for eXtreme Gradient Boosting, is a powerful machine learning algorithm known for its speed and performance in handling large datasets. It is widely used in both industry and academia for a variety of tasks, including classification, regression, and ranking.

One of the key features of XGBoost is its ability to handle missing values in the dataset, making it a robust choice for real-world data that often contains incomplete information. This algorithm also includes regularization techniques to prevent overfitting and improve generalization performance.

XGBoost is based on the concept of boosting, where multiple weak learners are combined to create a strong learner. The algorithm works by iteratively adding new models to the ensemble, with each new model focusing on the mistakes made by the previous models. This iterative process allows XGBoost to continuously improve its predictive performance.

In addition to its speed and performance, XGBoost also provides useful insights into the importance of features in the dataset. By analyzing the feature importance scores generated by the algorithm, users can gain a better understanding of which variables are most influential in making predictions.

Overall, XGBoost is a versatile and powerful machine learning algorithm that is well-suited for a wide range of tasks. Whether you are working on classification, regression, or ranking problems, XGBoost is a reliable choice that can help you achieve accurate and reliable results.

Chapter 13: Conclusion

Summary of Key Points

Summary of Key Points:

In this comprehensive guide to machine learning frameworks, we have covered a wide range of topics to provide you with a comprehensive overview of the field. From deep learning to reinforcement learning, natural language processing to computer vision, transfer learning to Bayesian machine learning, we have delved into the key concepts and frameworks that are essential for anyone working in the field of machine learning.

One of the key takeaways from this guide is the importance of choosing the right framework for your specific project or application. Different frameworks excel in different areas, whether it be speed, accuracy, ease of use, or scalability. By understanding the strengths and weaknesses of each framework, you can make an informed decision on which one is best suited for your needs.

Another important point to consider is the growing trend towards autoML frameworks, which automate the process of machine learning model selection, training, and optimization. These frameworks are making it easier than ever for non-experts to leverage the power of machine learning in their own projects, without the need for extensive knowledge or experience in the field.

Federated learning frameworks are also gaining traction in the machine learning community, as they enable training models on decentralized data sources without the need to centralize the data. This approach is particularly useful in scenarios where data privacy and security are paramount, such as in healthcare or financial industries.

Overall, this guide serves as a comprehensive roadmap for anyone looking to navigate the complex landscape of machine learning frameworks. Whether you are a seasoned machine learning practitioner or a beginner looking to get started, this guide provides a wealth of information to help you on your journey towards mastering the field of machine learning.

Future Trends in Machine Learning Frameworks

As the field of machine learning continues to evolve at a rapid pace, it is important for practitioners to stay abreast of the latest trends in frameworks that can help them build and deploy models more efficiently. In this subchapter, we will explore some of the future trends in machine learning frameworks that are shaping the industry.

The Complete Guide to AI Frameworks: A Comprehensive Overview

One of the key trends that we are seeing in machine learning frameworks is the move towards more user-friendly and accessible tools. As machine learning becomes more mainstream, there is a growing demand for frameworks that are easy to use and require minimal coding knowledge. This trend is driving the development of tools that allow users to build and deploy models with just a few clicks, making machine learning more accessible to a wider audience.

Another trend that is shaping the future of machine learning frameworks is the integration of deep learning capabilities. Deep learning has revolutionized the field of machine learning in recent years, allowing for more complex and accurate models to be built. As a result, many frameworks are now incorporating deep learning capabilities into their toolkits, enabling users to take advantage of this powerful technology in their own projects.

Reinforcement learning is also becoming an increasingly important area of focus in machine learning frameworks. This type of learning, which involves training models through a system of rewards and punishments, has shown great promise in a wide range of applications, from robotics to gaming. As a result, we are seeing more frameworks that support reinforcement learning, making it easier for practitioners to incorporate this technique into their own projects.

In addition to deep learning and reinforcement learning, natural language processing (NLP) is another area where we are seeing significant advancements in machine learning frameworks. NLP is a branch of artificial intelligence that focuses on the interaction between computers and humans through natural language. With the rise of chatbots, virtual assistants, and other NLP applications, there is a growing demand for frameworks that can support these technologies. As a result, we are seeing more frameworks that are specifically designed for NLP tasks, making it easier for practitioners to build and deploy models in this area.

Overall, the future of machine learning frameworks is bright, with a wide range of tools and technologies that are shaping the industry. By staying informed about the latest trends and developments in frameworks, practitioners can ensure that they are using the most cutting-edge tools to build and deploy models in their own projects. Whether you are interested in deep learning, reinforcement learning, NLP, computer vision, transfer learning, Bayesian machine learning, GANs, AutoML, federated learning, or time series analysis, there is a framework out there that can help you achieve your goals.

Final Thoughts

As we come to the end of this comprehensive guide on machine learning frameworks, it is important to reflect on the wealth of information that has been presented. From deep learning to reinforcement learning, natural language processing to computer vision, transfer learning to Bayesian machine learning, and everything in between, we have covered a wide range of topics in the field of machine learning. This guide is designed for people who want a deep understanding of the various frameworks available and how they can be applied in different contexts.

One key takeaway from this guide is the importance of choosing the right framework for the task at hand. With so many options available, it can be overwhelming to decide which framework to use. However, by understanding the strengths and weaknesses of each framework, you can make an informed decision that will ultimately lead to better results in your machine learning projects. Whether you are working on a time series analysis project or delving into the world of generative adversarial networks, having a solid understanding of the available frameworks is essential.

Another important point to consider is the rapidly evolving nature of machine learning frameworks. New frameworks are constantly being developed, and existing frameworks are being updated with new features and improvements. It is crucial to stay up-to-date with the latest developments in the field in order to remain competitive and continue producing cutting-edge machine learning solutions. This guide is meant to provide a solid foundation of knowledge, but it is important to continue learning and exploring new frameworks as they emerge.

The Complete Guide to AI Frameworks: A Comprehensive Overview

In conclusion, machine learning frameworks are powerful tools that can help you unlock the full potential of your data. By understanding the various frameworks available and how they can be applied, you can create innovative solutions to complex problems and drive business growth. Whether you are a seasoned machine learning practitioner or just starting out in the field, this guide is meant to serve as a comprehensive resource to help you navigate the ever-changing landscape of machine learning frameworks. We hope that you have found this guide to be informative and valuable, and we wish you success in all your future machine learning endeavors.